Preambles and other poems

Preambles

and other poems

ALVIN FEINMAN

New York   Oxford University Press

1964

For Deborah

Contents

Preambles and other poems

I

Preambles

I

Vagrant, back, my scrutinies
The candid deformations as with use
A coat or trousers of one now dead
Or as habit smacks of certitude

Even cosmographies, broad orchards
The uncountable trees   Or a river
Seen along the green monotonies
Of its banks   And the talk

Of memorable ideals ending
In irrelevance   I would cite
Wind-twisted spaces, absence
Listing to a broken wall

And the cornered noons
Our lives played in, such things
As thwart beginnings, limit   Or
Juxtapose that longest vision

A bright bird winged to its idea
To the hand stripped
By a damaged resolution
Daily of its powers   *Archai*

Bruited through crumbling masteries
To hang like swollen apples
In the river, witnesses
Stilled to their clotted truth   All

Discursion fated and inept
So the superior reality
Of photographs   The soul's
Tragic abhorrence of detail.

II

Only, if then, the ordered state
The storied sentiment of rest
Of the child hand in the father's
Rigored, islands tethered

To complicit seas, and tempering
Winds to lull the will
To evidence, to the ripe profit
Of perfections, gardens

Rhyming the space we walk in
Harmony of season and design   So
Statues hold through every light
The grave persuasive

Candors of their stride   And so
The mind in everything it joins
And suffers to redeem apart
Plays victim to its own intent

Divines generics blooded
To its needs   The sculptor
Lending outward in his stroke
To each defeat a signature

The just reconnaissance
That even fruit, each excellence
Confirms its course   A leisure
As of sap or blood arrested

Only once and to the prime
Its issue vivifies   A sun
Luring the divisioned calms
The days extended under it.

III

But only loosed or salient
Out of this unbinding stream
The stain of dyings seen
On pavements and on blurted

Slopes of ground   As there
Where your farthest reach
Is lived of want or membership
The ranged and slackened traffics

Cease   A bird in mid-flight
Falls, let silence, hair
The credible of touch adventure
There   Or certain laughters

Freedoms and the heat
Of only arms and of the thighs
These even love's rejoinder
As of every severed thing

The *ecce* only, only hands
Or hardnesses, the gleam a water
Or a light, a paused thing
Clothes in vacua killed

To a limbless beauty   Take
These torn possessives there
Where you plead the radiant
Of your truth's gloom   Own

To your sleep, your waking
The tread that is walked
From the inner of its pace
The play of a leaf to an earth.

Old World Travelogue

Back and late the northern valleys
And the carved centers of the west
Pitiably risen in flat places,
Their space, their calendar, a name
Affixed to treaties, distinctly ending:

The last stop, the wide sense of the edge.
Even these sure and splendid differences
Will mimic them, the wiser seemings
Of an open south, a mystery of flesh
More real, and incommutable—

Still in those starks the lungs will stumble,
Start to a skyline's baffled summoning:
One who strays at a rubbled limit,
Leans to a river and river-lights,
Hair blown, the spell of bridges . . .

Spurned divisions that will not close,
Gather to a claim, let the will relent:
So streets encountered in a guileless sun,
Words shaped to their translated sense,
A life contrived in a warmer country.

Landscape (Sicily)

I have seen your steeples and your lands
Speared by awkward cactuses and long birds
Flatten your yellow stones, your worn mountains.

Surely where those hills spilled villages
Toward the sea I should have wanted
Savagery, a touch icier than physical sport;

But vegetation withered from a forest
Of inconclusive starts, memory only
Gathered to a shade in the sun-sorrowed square.

A shade, sun-struck, whose hold will cover
The play of boys in blood-red clothing
And call your seasons to a wall of flatted rhythms,

To a slow summit of retreating days, days
Like winds through given linen, through dust.
These green reductions of your ancient freedoms—

The stunted olive, the lizard fixed
In soundless grasses, your yellow stones
Rubbed by the moon, the moon-quelled beaches,

And all asceticisms grown separate, skilled
To plump intrinsic endings—the fig-tree's
Sudden, rounded fingers; history

At the close will cripple to these things:
A body without eyes, a hand, the vacant
Presence of unjoined, necessary things.

II

Pilgrim Heights

Something, something, the heart here
Misses, something it knows it needs
Unable to bless—the wind passes;
A swifter shadow sweeps the reeds,
The heart a colder contrast brushes.

So this fool, face-forward, belly
Pressed among the rushes, plays out
His pulse to the dune's long slant
Down from blue to bluer element,
The bold encompassing drink of air

And namelessness, a length compound
Of want and oneness the shore's mumbling
Distantly tells—something a wing's
Dry pivot stresses, carved
Through barrens of stillness and glare:

The naked close of light in light,
Light's spare embrace of blade and tremor
Stealing the generous eye's plunder
Like a breathing banished from the lung's
Fever, lost in parenthetic air.

Raiding these nude recesses, the hawk
Resumes his yielding balance, his shadow
Swims the field, the sands beyond,
The narrow edges fed out to light,
To the sea's eternal licking monochrome.

The foolish hip, the elbow bruise
Upright from the dampening mat,
The twisted grasses turn, unthatch,
Light-headed blood renews its stammer—
Apart, below, the dazed eye catches

A darkened figure abruptly measured
Where folding breakers lay their whites;
The heart from its height starts downward,
Swum in that perfect pleasure
It knows it needs, unable to bless.

The Sun Goes Blind

The sun goes blind against my hand,
I lay the blue surrender of a bay
Down the burning corner of my reach.

The clouds retard and turn and catch,
Their casuistries cannot detain
The monody I move them through.

I let one silent flank alone
Of grazing pine encroach upon
The helmed embankments of my air.

Nameless, some quick or yellow bird
Finds me too wide to thread to flight,
Too still from bough to fretful bough.

Earth presses me in cramped duress—;
It is too gross a weight to be
Withheld, to labor forth—
                              this
Weight itself of weightlessness.

Scene Recalled

How should I not have preferred
The flinted salt of occasion?

The stern
Adequation I required of my eye:

A time
Of gulls riding out,
Of the tide going cold at my ankles;

A scene
Held tall as postponement,
As authority printed to landscape.

You are not the first man who exacted
Of flight it ascend through his shoulder;

Through the copper of nightfall the silver.

Solstice

Instance, the fire
that is in these facts, the burning
bearing into every edge
across the calm that
bridges them
                here
is it, the central all
slumped in the sun
breezing itself its mid-day fever

a spire
is off, or fraught
awash, no special
grass but flat and porch
                    and only
jackbird sulks in his tree
the fire of his silence in me.

Snow

Now sudden, or again, this easy
Quieter. You will know its fall
And what it lies on,
All, sign, metal, tar
One long and skeletal reductum

As, but warm, this side the pane
You purchase sense for.
But the gods give down
Chill unities, the pulver of an under-
Lying argument, assuager

Of nothing nameable: you know
The light snow holds and what
Its bodyable shape
Subdues, the gutter of all things
A virgin unison; and how

The glass that frames this waste
Of contour lames to blur
The baffled figure
To the drift he scurries through
—Blear hazarder. More bold,

The discrepant mind will break
The centrum of its loss,
Sudden and again,
Mistake its signature, as though
Snow were its poem out of snow.

Waters

Sunlight stitching the water—
an oar silverly lifted.
And blue, and yellow, and red boats drift—
like pleasures in a mind that needs no center.

One and one
leaves scuff into the lake and stop
drily as swans exchange their motions.

Last year's leaves. And boys
—stopping and starting
among the new vague blazes of the trees,
yellow, and suggested green—have now
a stiffened squirrel hung upon a stick
and lower him
with the firm excitement of natural action

his quick and singular attentions, all
that green and ragged round of starts
slipped under sieving waters.

Waters (2)

Broad emptiness of waters watched
      dull slant of light
      the roused abeyances of earth

So Chinese paintings
      not correcting the world
      invoke world-absences

Importantly
      because a breathing serves these pauses
      as though we were alone
      all birds south

      our loyalties renewing.

Earths and Sorrows

Grasses like knives and drilled
By the roots strangled   The upward
Downward tearings, and the dread
Irresistible sucking at a bruised
Defenseless sex   This remorseless
Forcing of a sickened ecstasy
                                        Earth
In her sensible labors pouring
The green extorted oils   Giving
Past shame   Or weeping   Or rejoicing

Let the winds consider
If these be the flower of her sorrow.

III

Relic

I will see her stand
half a step back of the edge of some high place
or at a leafless tree in some city park
or seated with her knees toward me and her face
        turned toward the window

And always the tips of the fingers of both her hands
will pull or twist at a handkerchief
like lovely deadly birds at a living thing
trying to work apart something exquisitely,
        unreasonably joined.

Three Elementary Prophecies

1. For Departure

You will not want what gives this going speech
Only as loss the stay of it
Not the rhythm drained into its sense
Like a world surviving

Only as absence, as a silence touched
A thing out of the body gone, desire
Or a blood-accustomed dread

Nor seek a knowledge of this breach
A name of it, as love
The flawless metamorphosis of dying
Stilled to its idea

Or membered like presentiment or choice
To your days' held mine
A sentence, or the letter of a truth

Only this presence destined
As a weather from its source
Toward broad or violent unleashings
Fables of the suffered and the joined

The rest unnumbered and devoid
A wind that will not move or pass
Rain tangled to a ruin, to
A season's felled forgotten root.

2. For Passage

Think then the ruin of your thoughts, and where
The persistent blood beats still under them,
Of birds you cannot follow with your eye.

Think the dark and breeding thickets
Where lowly animals die, and over the gloom
Bright birds passing in the light:

"What is your life if not the flashed stroke
Of your meaning, of water
Hurled once or blindly against rock,

Your living laid to the pillow of its sleep
As windows close to the street's tumult,
To love's long minute and the lips . . ."

Nail your will to the yellow fallings
Of your days, as tragedies slip
Their herald warnings through their acts.

Own land and sky, all seeing suffering things,
Water riding water, wing and roof,
The rip and baggage of all your ways.

3. For Return

Far, the farthest exile, and the steed
You ride must paw the ground, riderless,
Death's resignation come to matter

To mercies walked from the same blue fulcrum
Where your powers impel you
Unobscured by necessary pities,
       hungers
Come like numbered birds in the common air
And needs before they improvise their names

There love will touch where your energies begin
Where your hand asks you light from primary colors,
Assembles a mystery detained by sorrows

Like roofs the color of particular houses
And the logic of unexpected trees, love
Like sons will be far in the night
Close, as horses in the night, and welcome.

What Land

What silence speaking enough—:
Salt arbors, Archangels of the sea
Have slipped through slow impendings
Past risen things (what speech within?)
Of terrible ripeness
Of wet defeatingness
(Is a dripping body *silent?*)
As the sea contains, if this were lived in the sea;
If this were life there illumined.

That Ground

What acid eats the blind clay smile,
The earth how far, pummeled
In soft rain odors.

Never will it be possible to illumine that ground,
But know how her breathing
Shapes the hapless arms of trees;

How hair exhumes a menace of boughs,
Unvisited radiants darkling in the leaf;

And the smile a voice abused in winds,
The lips made possible
In virtue of silence,
Of the new distance of the earth.

This Face of Love

Nor prospect, promise   solely such
Breathed honey   as in breathing
Clamps the lung   and lowers life
Into this death   the very dying
Meaning of that breath   that beats
To black and beating honey   in an air
Thrown knowledgeless   imageless
Or only the wet hair   across her eyes.

For the Child Unanswered in Her

What scene, what street you started from
Is not abolished:
Stairwell, day-rise, long intonation of rain
        and piano,
And the dreamt animal meadow—
All laid waste, even at hair's breadth pierceable.

Child-heart, the illegible promise
Is not delivered in natural thickness
Of star and belly-loam.

Here by consummate gravities
Walls that have done and nothing
Pleads entrance to the mother arm:

                —O listen,
The splendid throat of every column
Aloud in the beating nipple.

Bridgelessly lit as the seed's leap,
Convene your gaze to the Mortal Brow
Always near, always unable to return your wish.

Relic (2)

Who can say we are wrong to fail the circuit of guesses—
For I enter for you the frail damage of these lights
(Dear one forgive a driven youth its steel forgeries).

What you desert now loses me haltingly,
Surely voyager where you are, and welcomed
To your trackless survival of eyes;

As by gracious rain, frail windows,
Your eyes' help for the bitter green of the leaves.

Relic (3)

Icarian instant O my love!
That, and the hell you are burned for—
Your inverted egypt of timelessness:
That the years are an endless arcade
Where horizon to horizon
The far-shot streamers of your fireworks
Never quite extinguish.

Responsibilities and Farewell

Final, irredeemable, all
Saw that, coming to themselves,
The equation, stunned, and good-bye.

All were entered, entrusted, spoken
To the end, cancelled.
                      Saw youth,
The secret ascetic, the gunner,
Broken of all littler love, taken—

Was it some fool head in a gutter
Spoiled the use of separable excellence;

Or blanks, or peaces, secrets of old men—
A shoe, a hat, a yellow, or a bench;

Or the eye of the human survivor?

Wiped of all but the whole desire,
Welcomed to the least all-seeing pleasure.

The End of the Private Mind

The end of the private mind
was in stone, in such thrifty thicknesses
including the connections
including the bits
                    —That
was the letting of it, it was not
obscure, but public as nails, as
stains in a flock of summery gutters

The death of it was generous
as it lived, only silly, and yet
not sillier, for Care
like an empty sleeve . . .
                    For Care,
a shy grass quiet in the cracks.

IV

Statuary   SIX POEMS

1.   Tags, or Stations

Tags, or stations, every bold
Approximate of everything, like leaves
The only pulp of what an autumn ought to be
Or landscape but the faltered posit,
Botched illation of a scenery;

Not this film and driven random
Purpose cannot bend, or take,
But what disarms the as-such of your aim
Pinned as were a street to the fake
Of direction only, only

The nisus of an argument, a hand
Fingered, nothing fingering, a word
The beating syllable of no word's voice
Or a footbeat no one walks toward
You, yourself the journey you rehearse.

2. All of This

All of this, the literal streets
Will never end, the steps, and pavement
Though you stop, or stop forever
Gripped to an immortal truth,
A word literal as one word only.

The flavor of this rain will lick you
Where you stand, where standing one
Or one emotion drowns your air:

You, where you are, eternal-eyed,
The apparition of what will, what iron
Archangel of its parable?

All this, the pavement, footsteps
And of rain, the long, the light of it
On metal, stone
                          —the throat's own violence
Deserts that cry, that silence
You, your posture, are perfected by.

3. Portrait

Ich bin ein Bild
Verlangt nicht dass ich rede.

I spoke, my voice sounded,
And I heard: —as things that pause
Are brightened, cleared by angers—
Anger by desire wounded.

Far, far up the land
I found a shoreline, birds
Standing and no sea
Slapping it, nor wind

But arrested things
I could not hear;
Angers bent by angers,
Breath in the lungs stunned.

And my throat still instinct
With its pleasure
Started and was still,
The vein swollen, intact.

4. Sentinel

How shall we know him now
Who comprehends but one
Compassion any more? A window
Darkened always onto this
Same street, whatever passes;
Or a street cut off, and all
Its passage, at the frame of that
Same vantage—
                  an ignorance
That stands as though it were a center
Which nothing various
Could enter, or ever hope
To plagiarize.

5.   L'Impasse des Deux Anges

Forget what route you travel here
To raise your outrage to the night—
Regard this now dead-ending square

Where two contrive one slant
Of combat locked, a boldness
Blind to the fury of its formal light.

Not all our sounded ways
Unculminate their single chord,
Not though we come tongue-humbled

Mumbling our meaning
Like deafened men, who trouble
Your arm, point where you cannot see

Nor seeing understand—
Regard these two, perpetual, firm,
Closed in struggle that cannot bend.

6.   Covenant

Some other side of memory
And nothing still to think;
The soul consumed a heaviness
Of thirst it couldn't drink.

A stone-like hand regards
The cramp to lift its sword;
A vigilance falls down
Invidiously loud.

The year undoes its pride,
An innocent-seeming form;
A length of natural days
Equivalently looms.

Street and star appear
(If distance can be true);
Another sense to pledge,
A blank page given you.

Noon

And something not themselves, a thing
That lags, or overbends, a white
That waits in tightly knuckled things . . .

The buildings hold their height,
The air itself its care
For clarity, for outline, for the flight
Of birds
          —as though an emptiness
Could fall, or fill all space
With some forgottenness: that thing
Out of which nothing knows itself . . .

In every gesture of the face, the hand,
What loss or trust is mastering its ground?

Great Stroke of Noon that does not sound.

True Night

So it is midnight, and all
The angels of ordinary day gone,
The abiding absence between day and day
Come like true and only rain
Comes instant, eternal, again:

As though an air had opened without sound
In which all things are sanctified,
In which they are at prayer—
The drunken man in his stupor,
The madman's lucid shrinking circle;

As though all things shone perfectly,
Perfected in self-discrepancy:
The widow wedded to her grief,
The hangman haloed in remorse—
I should not rearrange a leaf,

No more than wish to lighten stones
Or still the sea where it still roars—
Here every grief requires its grief,
Here every longing thing is lit
Like darkness at an altar.

As long as truest night is long,
Let no discordant wing
Corrupt these sorrows into song.

Annus Mirabilis

Year of wonder, the virgin
Gleam and scent of oil
Of the olive, of the year
Cool and hushed and overall
Wine stops in the belly
Sheep puzzle the hillside
Begun looking, animals
Close toward the smell of angel

Hand petals breast, the virgin
Invents of womanly gesture
Hand disposed backward
Toward the hand of a child
Green and brown and stone
Connoiter, trees marry
Air, a bird alights
And is still, wings
Ruffle and are still, leaf
Holds color and the moon
Maintains phase and shadow

All things disassume
Their motions, flesh and
Memoryless moduli of sense
Winds die to edens of standing
Weather, nudities reestablish
As a sleeper wakes
As a trance resumes
A wrist holds thought
Of imminence, never.

Mythos

Shaping adventures where there are none
Back out of waiting, of return
The told assembles these lenient energies:
    A dwelling entered,
        A garment flung away.

Slack and image suffer to a sense
As limbs perfect a motive of their grip,
Possibility stained to a personal color:
    The sleepers dream,
        Dreamt by another's touch.

The plot will triumph where there is no plot,
The hero bedded in his stars
Show character at last candescent in its wake:
    Dawn rendered to a face,
        The night to a sounding dog.

Mythos (2)

Enter: each scrap of narrative
Defeated into weather. Sudden
As a light's importance, or a light
Shammed to the space intention seeks—
Committing stride against the walk
Of forward's amble, forward's ease
Frozen, finding the wind's lone tongue,
The hungering stopped ear: again, again, again.

The mind is slow, lets slip
This savage of its grasp. Mind
Knows itself diviner than it makes,
As pace is always disparate, inept
Against the light traversed things hold—:

All violences stayed and sudden light,
All pantomime and reason flayed
Between two edges:
                        life leaves its stories,
These this leaving take and live
The lease they claim, repeat the wind's
Unsunderable sweeps, the eager leaves
And the light again lingering in its place.

Visitations, Habitats

Visitations, habitats, hard and sundry
Currencies of sense which can stay, not
By reminiscence or redundancy, but as
Encounter strands a voice, or battle-
Scenes detain a color and a face

Outside the campaign's vigor or the war's
Result, such rigors of the mediate
Against all end: as here the arrow
Of your kiss uniquely blinds
Through the bright sorrows of all our days

Tell me that mind, the longest realism
Of now or will is powerless to speak
Direction of forgetfulness, or distance
Change; that the severest task
Will always be what truth we put

The twisting present to; that the man
Who holds you is the boy whom the sun
Burdens, whose loyalties grow dumb
Surviving dangers: as now to narrow
To your hair the fear no vow,

Not love's devoutest tyranny may fuse
Stray voices, no result of sorrows
Nor any message join those faces
Which resume each morning separately
To bleed unvaryingly the echo, the demand

Into every original or accumulated sun,
To borrow the most mated destinations
Of all bliss, the fear that broken
Splendor breaks us where we live, the life
We gather to our life we never own at all.

V

November Sunday Morning

And the light, a wakened heyday of air
Tuned low and clear and wide,
A radiance now that would emblaze
And veil the most golden horn
Or any entering of a sudden clearing
To a standing, astonished, revealed . . .

That the actual streets I loitered in
Lay lit like fields, or narrow channels
About to open to a burning river;
All brick and window vivid and calm
As though composed in a rigid water
No random traffic would dispel . . .

As now through the park, and across
The chill nailed colors of the roofs,
And on near trees stripped bare,
Corrected in the scant remaining leaf
To their severe essential elegance,
Light is the all-exacting good,

That dry, forever virile stream
That wipes each thing to what it is,
The whole, collage and stone, cleansed
To its proper pastoral . . .
                                    I sit
And smoke, and linger out desire.

Stare at the Sea

Stare at the sea, the sea is blind.
The sea gives back your theme—
The sea that is not like, that cannot lack
A thing
            —you have heard this sea intoned
To every shock of chaos and of calm,
As though soul's torn two intellects
Would marry in that hollow heave
The harm they cannot fatalize, the thing
A stonier dumb charm would weave
Out of its own locked raging tides:
The sea holds nothing it can hide.

Teach the sea to sing, the soul
To drink its own imagining.

Swathes of March

Swathes of March, these days
And airs a high, thin shade of flint
—Important, personal, to go in your coat:
In the square a smoking chill, a light
That does not locate the sun;
And everything crossing, tree or life,
On its own, everything
Exactly inched toward an old exciting tooth
Of promise
        —Remembering your hair
        reverse the wind . . . Struck
That everything, everything
Writes into the clear middle of a page;
That never is there a place that is not
The miraculously turned margin of our lives.

Stills: From a 30th Summer

Shadow on a pavement,
　　sunlit street,
smear of rainbow
　　at the curb—
time is longer than the thought,
the playing out in slow.

Tangle of green grasses
　　holds a page,
leaf-weakened light
　　prints through—
What year of days has still to burn
before the stain wins through?

Poison of starlight
　　on the sill,
love spilled over
　　in the room—
life is everything it had to lose,
the losses broken into bloom.

On page 55, line 6 should read

the playing out is slow.

Late Light

Gracious this candid pair of eyes—
I stir my cup, and let
the grain lie liquid.

Outside, the steam that rises
from tracks the gravel cannot hold
has entered a shade of the light.

Light I remember seeing
at a dry enduring stairwell,
an abandoned flight of stairs.

Day, Daylong

Day, daylong, how the soul goes staring
At its shoes, expanse that widens nakedly
To world
           where each is poised
Assassin, suicide, to plead
Salvation of the other in its choice: yours
The helpless span narration cannot close.

Route nor spectacle will not go blind
Nor bind their broken conscience to a page:
Learn to be No-one in the voice of none,
Friend in that friendless element forever
Unbegun, a sea, a body, a remorse—

Take up this leaf: what do the dead,
The unborn defend? Your living syllable
Too mute, too loyal to its desuetude
To enter speech that does not speak
Consent, and claim, and failure to conclude.

Double Poem of Night and Snow

I

All, and more, still given, given you:
Each light that lames the avenue, the snow
That still can come to spaces veritably worn,
Long not your own. As though you slept. Or I
Sleep's sleeplessness to count without answer:
"Cold" and "street" and "star"—that where you wake
Or overtake me, nothing here resolve
To less than that these are.

II

Even in this light, these many points of light
That pierce the avenue, where weakly
A thin endeavor of snow sifts down: this thing
That goes and goes toward no root
                                    which rises—;
Even here whole candor fails, the cold
Is but your fever's brow: each lamp,
Pinpoint and aureole together flare.

Circumferences

Dawn under day, or dawning, lake, late edge,
Assumptive pure periphery where one thrust prominence
Now gives me back my eyes, my stride almost
A next abode, and source   O gathering, your smile
Is softer and more slow than the guileless surf
Drying forever at a farthest shore: I
Who have called you upright, destiny, or wall,
—How we exchange circumferences within
The one footfall that bruises us asunder.